My Clock Is Sick

Written by Emily Beth Gerard
Illustrated by David Slonim

"Oh, no," said Jack, "my clock is sick!"

"Get the doctor quick, quick, quick!"

"It doesn't tock.
It doesn't tick."

"Get the doctor quick, quick, quick!"

"It doesn't tock?
It doesn't tick?"

"Your clock is not sick, sick, sick."

"Plug it in quick, quick, quick!"